Fair Isle Mittens

LEISURE ARTS, INC.
Maumelle, Arkansas

Meet Lori Adams

Crocheting is my passion. If I'm holding still, I'm usually crocheting….. church, visiting friends, when in line at the grocery store, and when out on the boat with my husband who is a hunting guide out of Sitka, Alaska. Although crocheting is my passion, I prefer the way knitting looks, so I'm always trying to find new ways to crochet something so it looks like it is knitted. When the local yarn shop in my area displayed a gorgeous pair of knitted fair isle mittens I just HAD to figure out a way to crochet a pair for myself. This book is the result of that quest. It includes 11 charted designs with step-by-step instructions. And, with just one chart you can make any size ranging from small to x-large just by changing what size of yarn or hook you use. The Fair Isle crochet technique is fun and not as challenging as it looks. And, it's so rewarding to watch these pretty designs develop as you crochet that you'll want use this book to make mittens for all of your friends and family!

Ben Adams Photography

Contents

Project Gallery

Houndstooth Fingerless Mitts with Cuff

Argyle Mitten without Cuff

Diamonds Texting Mitten without Cuff

Hearts Mitten without Cuff   Snowflakes Mitten without Cuff

Hugs & Kisses Mitten with Cuff

Fish Skeleton Mitten without Cuff

Plaid Mitten without Cuff
Simple Dots Texting Mitten without Cuff

3-Color Argyle Mitten without Cuff

Stars & Stripes Mitten without Cuff

Here is a guide for the approximate amount of yarn and size hook needed to make one pair of full length Mittens (without cuffs), unlined or lined in the four sizes.

Yarn/Gauge/Hook Chart

YARN TYPE	GAUGE SWATCH (20 sts and 9 rnds)	SIZE	SUGGESTED YARNS	YARDS (METERS)
Super Fine Sock 7-8 sts = 1" (2.5 cm)	C2/2.75 mm 3¼"w x 1¼"h (8.25 cm x 3.25 cm)	Child/Small (unlined)	Red Heart - Heart & Sole Sock Yarn Premier - Serenity Sock Yarn	MC - 210 (192) CC - 210 (192)
Super Fine Sock 7-8 sts = 1" (2.5 cm)	D3/3.25 mm 3½"w x 1¼"h (9 cm x 3.25 cm)	Child/Small (lined)	Red Heart - Heart & Sole Sock Yarn Premier - Serenity Sock Yarn Lining - Red Heart Heart & Sole Sock Yarn Lining - Serenity Sock Yarn	MC - 210 (192) CC - 210 (192) Lining - 150 (137)
Fingering/ Sock 6-7 sts = 1" (2.5 cm)	D3/3.25 mm 3½"w x 1½"h (9 cm x 3.75 cm)	Teen/Medium (unlined)	Patons - Kroy Socks Patons - Kroy Socks FX	MC - 230 (210) CC - 230 (210)
Fingering/ Sock 6-7 sts = 1" (2.5 cm)	E4/3.5 mm 3¾"w x 1½"h (9.5 cm x 3.75 cm)	Teen/Medium (lined)	Patons - Kroy Socks Patons - Kroy Socks FX Lining - Red Heart Heart & Sole Sock Yarn Lining - Serenity Sock Yarn	MC - 230 (210) CC - 230 (210) Lining - 200 (183)
DK/Sport 5-6 sts = 1" (2.5 cm)	E4/3.5 mm 4¼"w x 1¾"h (10.75 cm x 4.5 cm)	Women's/ Large (unlined)	Lion Brand - LB Collection Superwash Merino or LB Collection Baby Alpaca Patons - Classic Wool DK Superwash	MC - 260 (238) CC - 260 (238)
DK/Sport 5-6 sts = 1" (2.5 cm)	F5/3.75 mm 4½"w x 1¾"h (11.5 cm x 4.5 cm)	Women's/ Large (lined)	Lion Brand - LB Collection Superwash Merino or LB Collection Baby Alpaca Patons - Classic Wool DK Lining - Kroy Socks or Kroy Socks FX	MC - 260 (238) CC - 260 (238) Lining - 220 (201)
Medium Weight 4-5 sts = 1" (2.5 cm)	F5/3.75 mm 4¾"w x 2"h (12 cm x 5 cm)	Men's/ X-Large (unlined)	Red Heart - Sheep Chic Merino Wool Yarn Lion Brand - Wool-Ease Yarn	MC - 280 (256) CC - 280 (256)
Medium Weight 4-5 sts = 1" (2.5 cm)	G6/4 mm 5"w x 2"h (12.75 cm x 5 cm)	Men's/ X-Large (lined)	Red Heart - Sheep Chic Merino Wool Yarn Lion Brand - Wool-Ease Yarn Lining - Lion Brand LB Collection Superwash Merino or LB Collection Baby Alpaca	MC - 280 (256) CC - 280 (256) Lining - 250 (229)

How to use this Book

1

Begin by picking a Mitten size from the Chart found on page 14. Note that the gauges are **different** between lined and unlined Mittens, so you need to make a decision on whether to line your Mittens **before** starting.

2

Make the Gauge Swatch on page 18 with the yarn and hook indicated for the size of Mitten you wish to crochet. If your gauge swatch isn't the size indicated, make another, changing the size of the hook until you find the size needed to obtain the gauge.

3

Determine which of the three types of Mittens you wish to make — regular Mittens, Fingerless Mitts or Texting Mittens. Since the Mittens are worked from fingertips to wrist, cuffs can be added as an option on all versions.

> Note that **all** sizes of the Mittens are made using the **same** instructions; the different sizes are obtained by using different hook sizes and weights of yarn.

Additional Supplies

Split-ring markers - see note under title of each individual style

Look for this-

> You will need 2 split-ring markers for this version.

Sewing thread and needle for Texting Mittens
4 buttons for Texting Mittens

Linings

We have provided 2 lining types.

Look for-

"LUMPY & BUMPY"

or

"SMOOTH"

Single Crochet Fair Isle Stitch
(split sc)

Always finish a split single crochet with the loop on your hook of the color you want the next stitch to be *(see Changing Colors, page 63)*. Lay the unused yarn color on top of your work loosely, so it will be covered by stitches. Instead of inserting your hook into the space under the two horizontal strands like a normal single crochet, insert the hook **between** the two vertical posts. While keeping the first loop on the hook fairly snug, pivot your hook upward so that the second loop on the hook will be slightly higher than the first loop. Keep the second loop loose as you yarn over with the color of the next stitch and draw through both loops on your hook, split sc complete *(Figs. 1-6)*.

Fig. 1

Hook indicating placement for an ordinary sc stitch (under the top 2 horizontal bars)

Fig. 2

Hook tip pointing to proper placement for split sc (**between** the 2 vertical posts)

Fig. 3

Insert hook **between** the 2 vertical posts and **under** the unused strand that was covered by the previous round.

Fig. 4

Yarn over and pull up a loop. Keep the first loop on the hook fairly

snug while using a pivoting motion to pull up the second loop slightly higher than the first loop. Note that the unused strand is laying loosely across the top of the work and is being covered with the stitches.

Fig. 5

The next stitch will be purple. The orange yarn is the "front" yarn, so it must cross over the top of the purple yarn which is the "back" yarn so it can stay in the front to avoid tangling.

Fig. 6

Yarn over with the purple yarn and draw through both loops on the hook. Note that crossing the orange "front" yarn over the top of the purple "back" yarn did not cause any tangles.

Tips for Success

Split single crochet stitches MUST be worked in a relaxed manner while pulling the second loop on the hook up slightly higher than the first loop and keeping it that way while finishing the stitch. If the second loop on the hook is not pulled up high enough, the spaces between the vertical posts will be too tight and your work will lean to the left. A little bit of leaning is inevitable and can be minimized with blocking once the mitten is done *(see Blocking, page 62)*, but a lot of leaning can not be fixed with blocking.

Working the gauge swatch on page 18 is the best way to practice and perfect the split single crochet stitch and learn how to follow a chart before making mittens *(see Following a Chart, page 62)*.

Unless you are proficient at holding multiple colors of yarn in one hand, you will have to set one yarn down and pick up the other each time you change colors. This may seem tedious at first, but as you see the beautiful pattern emerging I think you'll find that it's worth the extra motion.

Each split single crochet stitch should be worked over the unused yarn strand, so there are no floats on the back. After being covered, the unused strand will often be visible, peeking out through the stitches. To prevent this, work each split single crochet stitch **between** the vertical posts while inserting the hook **under** the unused strand

> ## Fair Isle Crochet is not very stretchy.
> Changing colors frequently in a round is the only thing that gives Fair Isle Crochet what little stretch it has. A round with very few color changes will be tighter than the rounds surrounding it because the unused yarn is running straight across the work. To prevent tight "bands" in your mittens from occurring, be sure to lay the unused strand LOOSELY across the top of your work, and maybe even stretch the work a little before changing colors so the unused strand pulls into the stitches covering it a little bit more, to provide as much stretch as possible.

covered by the previous round. This ensures that each strand of unused color is covered by TWO split single crochet stitches.

The unused strand of yarn is not always easy to find from the front of your work, but often you can see it better if you look at the back. For best results, glance at the back of your work while working every stitch. Sometimes during color changes or increases, the unused color strand is tucked down low or pulled up high where you can't readily find it. If you are unable to insert your hook under this strand, your stitch might ride up higher and tighter than the surrounding stitches and create a hole. So, be sure to keep your stitches loose enough that they look like the surrounding stitches for a nice, even professional look.

Don't get discouraged if your mittens have some "peek-a-boo" stitches where a second color shows through. I've noticed mittens that have been blocked and worn for even a short period of time tend to have yarn that "swells up," making most of the peek-a-boo stitches disappear.

Each ball of yarn should be specifically placed so that each color always enters the work from a separate angle to prevent tangling.

FOR EXAMPLE—place the darker yarn close to your hip and place the lighter yarn close to your knee, and keep them there. Pick up and set down the color by your knee in the back of your work. Pick up the color by your hip in the front, and set it down in the front by crossing it over your work. Even though this technique forces you to cross one color over the other and looks like you are creating knots in your work, once the stitches are completed, they relax and any potential knots disappear. Using this fixed placement method will save you hours of untwisting yarn balls.

Gauge Swatch

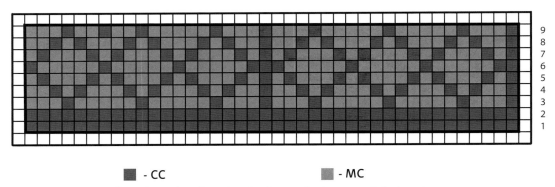

■ - CC   ■ - MC

Follow the color Chart beginning at the bottom right hand corner.

Work a gauge swatch and practice the Single Crochet Fair Isle Stitch (*Figs. 1-6, page 16*).

With hook indicated for yarn weight and CC, ch 40 **loosely**.

Rnd 1 (Right side): Working in back ridge of each ch (*Fig. 13, page 63*) and being careful **not** to twist; sc in first ch made (40th ch from hook), place marker around sc just made to indicate the beginning of rnd (*see Markers, page 62*), sc in each ch around; do **not** join.

Now it's time to add the second color even if the color chart does not yet indicate that it is time to be used. Rounds that are worked with only one strand of yarn are distinctly different in thickness and color from rounds that are worked with two strands, so it's very important to use two strands on **all** rounds. If the color chart indicates the use of a new color right away, just set down the unused color and draw a loop of the new color through both loops on the hook, then lay the tail of the new color across the top of your work alongside the unused color strand. If the color chart indicates a second color isn't going to be used immediately, add it anyway by laying the tail of the unused color across the top of your work, covering it with stitches until needed.

Leaving a very short end, **loosely** lay MC on top of Rnd 1.

Rnd 2: Working **over** MC, insert hook in marked sc, YO and pull up a loop slightly higher than loop on hook using a pivoting motion and keeping first loop fairly snug on the hook, YO and draw through both loops on hook to complete sc. Place a split-ring marker **between** vertical posts of st just made to mark placement of first split sc on next rnd (**now and throughout**), sc in each sc around in same manner, keeping unused color loosely on top of sts so it does not create a tight band around the piece.

Rnd 3: Insert hook **between** vertical posts of marked st and **under** unused MC strand on Rnd 2, with CC, YO and pull up a loop slightly higher than loop on hook using a pivoting motion and keeping first loop fairly snug on the hook. Drop CC and pick up MC, each from its proper position to reduce tangling. Make sure the unused CC yarn is laying **loosely** across the top of previous rnd, with MC, YO and draw through both loops on hook (**color changed and first split sc completed**). The unused CC strand is covered with a stitch and the loop on the hook is the correct color for the next stitch. Following Chart for color changes, work split sc around (*see Following a Chart, page 62 and Changing Colors, page 63*).

Remember to insert the hook **under** the unused yarn strand that was carried across the top of the previous round as often as possible with each stitch. This will encase the unused yarn strand twice, preventing it from being seen. If you're finding it difficult to push your hook through your work, you are crocheting too tightly. The split sc needs to be worked with a very relaxed hand.

Rnds 4-9: Following Chart, work split sc around.

Cut yarn leaving a 3" (7.5 cm) end, finish off.

Measure the swatch and count the stitches and rounds to find your gauge. Check the Yarn/Gauge/Hook Chart on page 14 for the gauge of the mitten size you are wanting to make. The whole hand of the wearer should slip through the circle without any problem. If you plan to line the mitten, the circle should be loose to allow room inside for a lining. If necessary, use a different size hook or yarn weight when making your mitten to achieve the proper size. Inspect the swatch and check to see if the stitches are gravitating to the left. A little bit of leaning is inevitable and can be minimized with blocking, but a lot of leaning is bad and can not be fixed with blocking.

You will notice on some of the designs that the ending stitches on a round and the beginning stitches on the next round do not match up *(Photo A)*. This is called "the dreaded jog" and can not be avoided when using the continuous round method.

Photo A

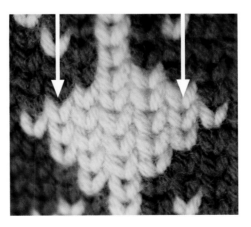

Mitten with Cuff

Follow Charts throughout (*see Following a Chart, page 62 and Changing Colors, page 63*).

You will need
2 split-ring markers
for this version.

SPLIT SINGLE CROCHET
(abbreviated split sc)
Insert hook **between** vertical posts of next st and **under** unused strand on previous rnd, YO and pull up a loop slightly higher than loop on hook using a pivoting motion while keeping first loop snug on the hook, YO and draw through both loops on hook **(split sc completed; *Figs. 1-6, page 16)***.

INCREASE (uses one st)
Work sc under both top loops of next st, work split sc **between** vertical posts of **same** st.

FRONT POST HALF DOUBLE CROCHET
(abbreviated FPhdc)
YO, insert hook from **front** to **back** around post of st indicated *(Fig. 17, page 63)*, YO and pull up a loop, YO and draw through all 3 loops on hook.

BACK POST HALF DOUBLE CROCHET
(abbreviated BPhdc)
YO, insert hook from **back** to **front** around post of st indicated *(Fig. 17, page 63)*, YO and pull up a loop, YO and draw through all 3 loops on hook.

FRONT POST SINGLE CROCHET *(abbreviated FPsc)*
Insert hook from **front** to **back** around post of st indicated *(Fig. 17, page 63)*, YO and pull up a loop, YO and draw through both loops on hook.

BACK POST SINGLE CROCHET *(abbreviated BPsc)*
Insert hook from **back** to **front** around post of st indicated *(Fig. 17, page 63)*, YO and pull up a loop, YO and draw through both loops on hook.

"The first rounds are difficult because they are small, the increases make the unused strand pull down out of sight and the color changes are awkward. Relax! If you get uptight and frustrated, your stitches will be too tight. Set your work down once in a while. It won't fall apart and you'll soon start to realize that you don't need to grip it to keep it intact. Take one stitch at a time. If you are struggling to get the hook into each stitch, you are working too tightly. You will need to loosen your tension or use a larger size hook."

MITTEN (Make 2)
THUMB
With first color indicated on desired Chart, ch 3 **tightly**, place marker around ch-3; join with slip st to form a ring with marker in center.

Rnd 1 (Right side)**:** Ch 1, sc **loosely** in ring, remove marker and place **between** vertical posts of sc just made to mark first st **and** the beginning of rnd *(see Markers, page 62)*, pull yarn end to back of work, work 7 sc **loosely** in ring; do **not** join: 8 sc.

Leaving a very short end, **loosely** lay second color on top of Rnd 1. Work over unused color throughout.

Rnd 2: Work split sc in marked st, remove marker and place **between** vertical posts of st just made **(now and throughout)**, work split sc, increase twice, work 2 split sc, increase twice: 12 sts.

Rnd 3: Work 2 split sc, increase, work split sc, increase, work 3 split sc, (increase, work split sc) twice: 16 sts.

Rnds 4-13: Work split sc around; at end of Rnd 13, complete last st by changing to same color as first st of rnd, remove marker. Drop loop from hook and place onto marker to keep piece from unraveling, cut same color leaving a 12" (30.5 cm) end and cut unused color leaving a 3" (7.5 cm) end. Set Thumb aside.

UPPER HAND

With first color indicated on Chart, ch 3 **tightly**, place marker around ch-3; join with slip st to form a ring with marker in center.

Rnds 1-3: Work same as Thumb: 16 sts.

Rnds 4-9: Following Chart, work split sc around working increases where indicated: 40 sts.

Rnds 10-29: Work split sc around.

Drop loop from hook and place onto marker; do **not** cut either yarn. Upper Hand complete.

THUMB JOINING

With **right** sides together, place Thumb and Upper Hand with the stitches to be joined together. Remove loop from Thumb marker and place on hook. Working from **wrong** side of Upper Hand, insert hook through st on Upper Hand and through st on Thumb *(Fig. 7)*.

Fig. 7

YO **tightly** and draw through sts and loop on hook, ch 1 **tightly**, finish off. Do **not** pull tightly on either strand of Thumb yarn or a tight "band" will form around the Thumb. The Thumb and the Upper Hand are joined into one piece.

LOWER HAND

Rnd 30: Place loop from Upper Hand marker onto hook. Working over yarn ends, work split sc in next split sc, place marker to indicate the beginning of rnd, work 19 split sc around Upper Hand, work split sc in same st as joining on Upper Hand, work split sc in same st as joining on Thumb, work 15 split sc around Thumb, work split sc in same st as joining on Thumb, work split sc in same st as joining on Upper Hand, work 19 split sc around Upper Hand: 58 split sc.

Rnd 31: Work 21 split sc, skip next split sc, work 15 split sc, skip next split sc, work 20 split sc: 56 split sc.

Rnd 32: Work 21 split sc, skip next split sc, work 13 split sc, skip next split sc, work 20 split sc: 54 split sc.

Rnd 33: Work split sc around.

Rnd 34: Work 21 split sc, skip next split sc, work 11 split sc, skip next split sc, work 20 split sc: 52 split sc.

Rnd 35: Work split sc around.

Rnd 36: Work 21 split sc, skip next split sc, work 9 split sc, skip next split sc, work 20 split sc: 50 split sc.

Rnd 37: Work split sc around.

Rnd 38: Work 21 split sc, skip next split sc, work 7 split sc, skip next split sc, work 20 split sc: 48 split sc.

Rnd 39: Work split sc around.

Rnd 40: Work 21 split sc, skip next split sc, work 5 split sc, skip next split sc, work 20 split sc: 46 split sc.

Rnds 41 and 42: Work split sc around.

Rnd 43: Work 21 split sc, skip next split sc, work 3 split sc, skip next split sc, work 20 split sc: 44 split sc.

Rnds 44 and 45: Work split sc around.

Rnd 46: Work 21 split sc, skip next split sc, work split sc, skip next split sc, work 20 split sc: 42 split sc.

Rnd 47: Work split sc around.

Rnd 48: Work 20 split sc, skip next split sc, work split sc, skip next split sc, work 19 split sc: 40 split sc.

Work even around until you reach the round marked "Stop for Cuff."

CUFF

Choose color for Cuff; cut unused color leaving a 3" (7.5 cm) end to work over.

Rnd 1: Work split sc in next split sc, move marker to Back Loop Only of st just made *(Fig. 14, page 63)*, working over yarn end, work split sc around.

Rnd 2: Working in Front Loops Only, sc in first split sc, leaving first marker in Back Loop Only for lining placement, place second marker to indicate beginning of rnd, sc in each split sc around.

The free loops of Rnd 1 are available to be used if you have decided to line the Mittens.

Rnd 3: Work FPsc around next sc, work BPsc around next sc, ★ work FPhdc around next sc, work BPhdc around next sc; repeat from ★ around.

Rnd 4: ★ Work FPhdc around next st, work BPhdc around next st; repeat from ★ around.

Repeat Rnd 4 for pattern until Cuff is desired length.

Last Rnd: ★ Work FPhdc around next st, work BPhdc around next st; repeat from ★ 18 times **more**, work BPsc around next st, work FPsc around next st; slip st in next st, finish off.

If you have decided not to line the Mittens, block them *(see Blocking, page 62)*.

If you have decided to line the Mittens, block them first *(see Blocking, page 62)*; then see "Lumpy & Bumpy" Lining, page 26 or "Smooth" Lining, page 28.

Mitten without Cuff

Follow Charts throughout *(see Following a Chart, page 62 and Changing Colors, page 63)*.

You will need
2 split-ring markers
for this version.

STITCH GUIDE

SLIP STITCH 2 TOGETHER
(abbreviated slip st2tog)
(uses next 2 split sc)
Insert hook in Front Loop Only of next 2 split sc *(Fig. 14, page 63)*, YO and draw though sts **and** loop on hook.

THUMB

Following desired Chart, work same as Mitten With Cuff, page 20.

UPPER & LOWER HAND

Rnds 1-48: Work same as Mitten With Cuff: 40 split sc.

Rnds 49-59: Work split sc around.

Rnd 60: Cut unused color leaving 3" (7.5 cm) end, work split sc in next st, place marker in Front Loop Only of st just made *(Fig. 14, page 63)*, working over yarn end, work split sc around.

Reverse direction by turning your work counterclockwise so you are working from the **inside** of the Mitten. This will feel awkward, but don't worry, it will look fine. Reversing direction ensures that the stitches in the next round will curl slightly toward the inside of the Mitten for a nice finish.

Rnd 61: Turn; skip next split sc, working in Front Loops Only, slip st in next split sc, place marker in st just made, (slip st in next 17 split sc, slip st2tog) twice, slip st in same st as marker, do **not** remove marker if planning on lining, finish off: 37 sts.

If you have decided not to line the Mittens, block them *(see Blocking, page 62)*.

The free loops of Rnd 60 are available to be used if you have decided to line the Mittens. Block them first *(see Blocking, page 62)*; then see "Lumpy & Bumpy" Lining, page 26 or "Smooth" Lining, page 28.

"SMOOTH"

"LUMPY & BUMPY"

"The Linings are essentially slightly smaller mittens that are attached to the bottoms of outer mittens that have been made a little bigger than the perfect fit. For best results, use a soft yarn that is a lighter weight than what you used for the outer mitten. If you do use yarn that is of the exact same weight as the outer mitten, use a smaller size hook than what you used for the outer mitten. Be sure to block your Mittens first before adding Lining (see Blocking, page 62)."

> You will need two split-ring markers for either of these Linings.

"LUMPY & BUMPY"

STITCH GUIDE

TREBLE CROCHET *(abbreviated tr)*
YO twice, insert hook in st indicated, YO and pull up a loop (4 loops on hook), (YO and draw through 2 loops on hook) 3 times.

HALF DOUBLE CROCHET 2 TOGETHER *(abbreviated hdc2tog)* (uses next 2 sts)
★ YO, insert hook in **next** st, YO and pull up a loop; repeat from ★ once **more**; YO and draw through all 5 loops on hook (**counts as one hdc**).

DECREASE (uses next 2 sts)
YO, insert hook in next st, YO and pull up a loop, YO and draw through 2 loops on hook, YO, insert hook in next st, YO and pull up a loop, YO and draw through all 4 loops on hook.

LOWER HAND

Flip Cuff up; hold the Mitten with fingertips pointing down, the Thumb toward you with the **wrong** side of the Mitten facing *(Fig. 8)*.

Fig. 8

The Lining's first round will be worked in the free loops of Rnd 1 on the Cuff *(Fig. 15a, page 63)*.

Rnd 1: Do **not** make a slip knot, insert hook in marked st, pull up a loop leaving a 3" (7.5 cm) end, YO and draw through loop on hook, sc in same st, remove marker and place in sc just made to indicate the beginning of rnd, working over yarn end, sc in next 11 sts, skip next st, (sc in next 12 sts, skip next st) twice, sc in next st: 37 sc.

Rnd 2: Sc in next st, (tr in next st, sc in next st) around.

Rnd 3: Tr in next sc, (sc in next tr, tr in next sc) around.

Rnds 4-6: Repeat Rnds 2 and 3 once, then repeat Rnd 2 once **more**; at end of Rnd 6, do **not** finish off, slip loop to marker to check the width.

Skip to Lining Width and work same as Mitten Without Cuff.

Hold the Mitten with fingertips pointing down, the Thumb toward you with the **wrong** side of the Mitten facing *(Fig. 9)*.

Fig. 9

The Lining's first round will be worked in the free loops of Rnd 60 *(Fig. 15a, page 63)*.

Rnd 1: Do **not** make a slip knot, insert hook in marked st, YO and pull up a loop leaving a 3" (7.5 cm) end, YO and draw through loop on hook, sc in same st, remove marker and place in sc just made to indicate the beginning of rnd, working over yarn end, sc in next 36 sts: 37 sc.

Rnd 2: Sc in next st, (tr in next st, sc in next st) around.

Rnd 3: Tr in next sc, (sc in next tr, tr in next sc) around.

Rnds 4-10: Repeat Rnds 2 and 3, 3 times; then repeat Rnd 2 once **more**; at end of Rnd 10, do **not** finish off, slip loop to marker to check the width.

LINING WIDTH

Fold the Lining up over the Mitten to check its size. It should be just slightly narrower than the Mitten. If the Lining is too wide or too narrow, you should try again using a different size hook or a different yarn weight. You can also increase or decrease the amount of stitches in multiples of 2. Be sure to note any changes to the pattern so there's no confusion when lining the second Mitten.

BOTTOM OF THUMB

Rnd 1: Tr in next sc, (sc in next tr, tr in next sc) 9 times, 2 hdc in next tr, tr in next sc, (sc in next tr, tr in next sc) 8 times: 38 sts.

Rnd 2: Sc in next tr, (tr in next sc, sc in next tr) 9 times, 2 hdc in each of next 2 hdc, sc in next tr, (tr in next sc, sc in next tr) 8 times: 40 sts.

Rnd 3: Tr in next sc, (sc in next tr, tr in next sc) 9 times, 2 hdc in next hdc, hdc in next 2 hdc, 2 hdc in next hdc, tr in next sc, (sc in next tr, tr in next sc) 8 times: 42 sts.

Rnd 4: Sc in next tr, (tr in next sc, sc in next tr) 9 times, 2 hdc in next hdc, hdc in next 4 hdc, 2 hdc in next hdc, sc in next tr, (tr in next sc, sc in next tr) 8 times: 44 sts.

Rnd 5: Tr in next sc, (sc in next tr, tr in next sc) 9 times, 2 hdc in next hdc, hdc in next 6 hdc, 2 hdc in next hdc, tr in next sc, (sc in next tr, tr in next sc) 8 times: 46 sts.

Rnd 6: Sc in next tr, (tr in next sc, sc in next tr) 9 times, 2 hdc in next hdc, hdc in next 8 hdc, 2 hdc in next hdc, sc in next tr, (tr in next sc, sc in next tr) 8 times: 48 sts.

Rnd 7: Tr in next sc, (sc in next tr, tr in next sc) 9 times, 2 hdc in next hdc, hdc in next 10 hdc, 2 hdc in next hdc, tr in next sc, (sc in next tr, tr in next sc) 8 times: 50 sts.

Rnd 8: Sc in next tr, (tr in next sc, sc in next tr) 9 times, 2 hdc in next hdc, hdc in next 12 hdc, 2 hdc in next hdc, sc in next tr, (tr in next sc, sc in next tr) 8 times: 52 sts.

Rnd 9 (Dividing rnd): Tr in next sc, (sc in next tr, tr in next sc) 9 times, insert hook in next hdc, YO and pull up a loop, skip next 14 hdc (Thumb hole), insert hook in next hdc, YO and pull up a loop, YO and draw though all 3 loops on hook (**counts as one sc**), place marker through **both** hdc worked into for st placement, tr in next sc, (sc in next tr, tr in next sc) 8 times: 37 sts.

UPPER HAND

Rnd 1: Sc in next tr, (tr in next sc, sc in next tr) around.

Rnd 2: Tr in next sc, (sc in next tr, tr in next sc) around.

Rnds 3-10: Repeat Rnds 1 and 2, 4 times.

LINING LENGTH

Before beginning the Shaping, check the Lining's length. A too long or too short lining can be very uncomfortable, so add or subtract rounds as needed for your size. Be sure to note any changes to the pattern so there's no confusion when lining the second Mitten.

SHAPING

Rnd 1: Decrease, (sc in next st, tr in next st) 7 times, decrease twice, sc in next st, (tr in next st, sc in next st) 7 times, decrease: 33 sts.

Rnd 2: Decrease, (sc in next st, tr in next st) 6 times, decrease twice, sc in next st, (tr in next st, sc in next st) 6 times, decrease: 29 sts.

Rnd 3: Decrease, (sc in next st, tr in next st) 5 times, decrease twice, sc in next st, (tr in next st, sc in next st) 5 times, decrease: 25 sts.

Rnd 4: Decrease, (sc in next st, tr in next st) 4 times, decrease twice, sc in next st, (tr in next st, sc in next st) 4 times, decrease: 21 sts.

Rnd 5: Decrease, (sc in next st, tr in next st) 3 times, decrease twice, sc in next st, (tr in next st, sc in next st) 3 times, decrease: 17 sts.

Closing: Fold last rnd flat with yarn at side edge, remove marker; working through **both** layers, slip st in each st across, cut yarn leaving 3" (7.5 cm) end; finish off, pull yarn end to inside of Lining, out of sight. Upper Hand Lining complete.

THUMB LINING

Hold the Mitten with the outer fingertips down, the Lining fingertips up and the Thumb to your left.

Rnd 1: Leaving a 3" (7.5 cm) end, with inside of Lining facing, insert hook through **both** marked sts, remove marker, YO and pull up a loop, ch 1, sc in same sp, place marker in sc just made to indicate the beginning of rnd, working over yarn end, hdc in each hdc around: 15 sts.

Rnds 2-5: Hdc in each st around.

Rnd 6: Hdc2tog, hdc in next 3 hdc, hdc2tog twice, hdc in next 4 hdc, hdc2tog: 11 hdc.

Rnd 7: Hdc2tog, hdc in next hdc, hdc2tog twice, hdc in next 2 hdc, hdc2tog: 7 hdc.

Closing: Complete same as Upper Hand Closing. Thumb Lining complete.

— "SMOOTH" —

LOWER HAND

 MITTEN WITH CUFF START HERE

Flip Cuff up; hold the Mitten with fingertips pointing down, the Thumb toward you with the **wrong** side of the Mitten facing (**Fig. 8, page 27**). The Lining's first round will be worked in the free loops of Rnd 1 on the Cuff (**Fig. 15a, page 63**).

Rnd 1: Do **not** make a slip knot, insert hook in marked st, YO and pull up a loop leaving a 3" (7.5 cm) end, YO and draw through loop on hook, sc in same st, remove marker and place in sc just made to indicate the beginning of rnd, working over yarn end, sc in next 11 sts, skip next st, (sc in next 12 sts, skip next st) twice, sc in next st: 37 sc.

Rnds 2-5: Sc in each sc around;

Rnd 6: Sc in next 18 sc, 2 sc in next sc, sc in next 18 sc; do **not** finish off, slip loop to marker to check the width: 38 sc.

Skip to Lining Width, page 29 and work same as Mitten Without Cuff.

MITTEN WITHOUT CUFF START HERE

Hold the Mitten with fingertips pointing down, the Thumb toward you with the **wrong** side of the Mitten facing *(Fig. 9, page 27)*. The Lining's first round will be worked in the free loops of Rnd 60 *(Fig. 15a, page 63)*.

Rnd 1: Do **not** make a slip knot, insert hook in marked st, YO and pull up a loop leaving a 3" (7.5 cm) end, YO and draw through loop on hook, sc in same st, remove marker and place in sc just made to indicate the beginning of rnd, working over yarn end, sc in next 36 sts: 37 sc.

Rnds 2-13: Sc in each sc around.

Rnd 14: Sc in next 18 sc, 2 sc in next sc, sc in next 18 sc: 38 sc.

Rnd 15: Sc in each sc around; do **not** finish off, slip loop to marker to check the width.

LINING WIDTH

Fold the Lining over the Mitten to check its size. It should be just slightly narrower than the Mitten. If the Lining is too wide or too narrow, you should try again using a different size hook or a different yarn weight. You can also increase or decrease the amount of stitches in multiples of 2. Be sure to note any changes to the pattern so there's no confusion when lining the second mitten.

BOTTOM OF THUMB

Rnd 1: Sc in next 18 sc, 2 sc in each of next 2 sc, sc in next 18 sc: 40 sc.

Rnd 2: Sc in each sc around.

Rnd 3: Sc in next 18 sc, 2 sc in next sc, sc in next 2 sc, 2 sc in next sc, sc in next 18 sc: 42 sc.

Rnd 4: Sc in each sc around.

Rnd 5: Sc in next 18 sc, 2 sc in next sc, sc in next 4 sc, 2 sc in next st, sc in next 18 sc: 44 sc.

Rnd 6: Sc in each sc around.

Rnd 7: Sc in next 18 sc, 2 sc in next sc, sc in next 6 sc, 2 sc in next st, sc in next 18 sc: 46 sc.

Rnd 8: Sc in each sc around.

Rnd 9: Sc in next 18 sc, 2 sc in next sc, sc in next 8 sc, 2 sc in next st, sc in next 18 sc: 48 sc.

Rnd 10: Sc in each sc around.

Rnd 11: Sc in next 18 sc, 2 sc in next sc, sc in next 10 sc, 2 sc in next st, sc in next 18 sc: 50 sc.

Rnd 12: Sc in each sc around.

Rnd 13: Sc in next 18 sc, 2 sc in next sc, sc in next 12 sc, 2 sc in next st, sc in next 18 sc: 52 sc.

Rnd 14 (Dividing rnd)**:** Sc in next 18 sc, insert hook in next sc, YO and pull up a loop, skip next 14 sc (Thumb hole), insert hook in next sc, YO and pull up a loop, YO and draw though all 3 loops on hook **(counts as one sc)**, place marker through **both** sc worked into for st placement, sc in next 18 sc: 37 sc.

UPPER HAND

Rnds 1-15: Sc in each sc around.

LINING LENGTH

Before beginning the Shaping, check the Lining's length. A too long or too short Lining can be very uncomfortable, so add or subtract rounds as needed for your size. Be sure to note any changes to the pattern so there's no confusion when lining the second Mitten.

SHAPING

Rnd 1: Skip next sc, sc in next 16 sc, skip next sc, sc in next sc, skip next sc, sc in next 15 sc, skip next sc, sc in next sc: 33 sc.

Rnd 2: Skip next sc, sc in next 14 sc, skip next sc, sc in next sc, skip next sc, sc in next 13 sc, skip next sc, sc in next sc: 29 sc.

Rnd 3: Skip next sc, sc in next 12 sc, skip next sc, sc in next sc, skip next sc, sc in next 11 sc, skip next sc, sc in next sc: 25 sc.

Rnd 4: Skip next sc, sc in next 10 sc, skip next sc, sc in next sc, skip next sc, sc in next 9 sc, skip next sc, sc in next sc: 21 sc.

Rnd 5: Skip next sc, sc in next 8 sc, skip next sc, sc in next sc, skip next sc, sc in next 7 sc, skip next sc, sc in next sc: 17 sc.

Rnd 6: Skip next sc, sc in next 6 sc, skip next sc, sc in next sc, skip next sc, sc in next 5 sc, skip next sc, sc in next sc: 13 sc.

Closing: Complete same as Upper Hand Closing on page 28.

THUMB LINING

Work same as Thumb Lining on page 28.

Fingerless Mitts

EASY +

Follow Charts throughout unless otherwise noted *(see Following a Chart, page 62 and Changing Colors, page 63)*.

You will need 3 split-ring markers for this version.

SPLIT SINGLE CROCHET
(abbreviated split sc)
Insert hook **between** vertical posts of next st and **under** unused strand on previous rnd, YO and pull up a loop slightly higher than loop on hook using a pivoting motion while keeping first loop snug on the hook, YO and draw through both loops on hook **(split sc completed; *Figs. 1-6, page 16*)**.

FRONT POST HALF DOUBLE CROCHET
(abbreviated FPhdc)
YO, insert hook from **front** to **back** around post of st indicated *(Fig. 17, page 63)*, YO and pull up a loop, YO and draw through all 3 loops on hook.

BACK POST HALF DOUBLE CROCHET
(abbreviated BPhdc)
YO, insert hook from **back** to **front** around post of st indicated *(Fig. 17, page 63)*, YO and pull up a loop, YO and draw through all 3 loops on hook.

FRONT POST SINGLE CROCHET
(abbreviated FPsc)
Insert hook from **front** to **back** around post of st indicated *(Fig. 17, page 63)*, YO and pull up a loop, YO and draw through both loops on hook.

BACK POST SINGLE CROCHET
(abbreviated BPsc)
Insert hook from **back** to **front** around post of st indicated *(Fig. 17, page 63)*, YO and pull up a loop, YO and draw through both loops on hook.

MITT (Make 2)
THUMB
RIBBING
Do **not** follow desired Thumb Chart until instructed.

With desired color, ch 16; do **not** join.

To work FPhdc in a ch, YO, insert hook from **front** to **back** into same ch as second leg of post st just made, then from **back** to **front** in next ch, YO and draw through all 3 loops on hook.

To work BPhdc in a ch, YO, insert hook from **back** to **front** into same ch as second leg of post st just made, then from **front** to **back** in next ch, YO and draw through all 3 loops on hook.

Rnd 1 (Right side)**:** Being careful not to twist, insert hook from **front** to **back** in first ch made (16th ch from hook), then from **back** to **front** in next ch, YO and pull up a loop, YO and draw through both loops on hook **(counts as first FPsc, now and throughout)**, place marker around st just made to indicate beginning of the round *(see Markers, page 62)*, insert hook from **front** to **back** in same ch as second leg of FPsc just made, then from **back** to **front** in next ch, YO and pull up a loop, YO and draw through both loops on hook **(counts as BPsc, now and throughout)**, (work FPhdc in ch, work BPhdc in ch) 7 times: 16 sts.

Rnd 2: Work FPhdc around next st, move marker to Back Loop Only of st just made *(Fig. 14, page 63)*, work BPhdc around next st, (work FPhdc around next st, work BPhdc around next st) 6 times, work FPsc around next st, work BPsc around next st.

Rnd 3: Working in Front Loops Only, sc in each st around, leave marker in place for Lining placement, place second marker to indicate beginning of rnd.

The free loops of Rnd 2 are available to be used later if you have decided to line the Mitts.

Leaving a very short end, **loosely** lay second color on top of Rnd 3. Work over unused color throughout.

Beginning at Rnd 13, follow desired Thumb Chart.

Rnd 13: With color indicated, sc in both loops of each sc around, completing last sc by changing to same color as first sc of rnd, remove marker. Drop loop from hook and place onto marker to keep piece from unraveling, cut same color leaving a 12" (30.5 cm) end and cut unused color leaving a 3" (7.5 cm) end. Set Thumb aside.

UPPER HAND
RIBBING
With same color as Thumb Ribbing, ch 40; do **not** join.

Rnd 1 (Right side)**:** Being careful not to twist, insert hook from **front** to **back** in first ch made (40th ch from hook), then from **back** to **front** in next ch, YO and pull up a loop, YO and draw through both loops on hook, place marker around FPsc just made to indicate

beginning of the round, insert hook from **front** to **back** in same ch as FPsc just made, then from **back** to **front** in next ch, YO and pull up a loop, YO and draw through both loops on hook, (work FPhdc in ch, work BPhdc in ch) 19 times: 40 sts.

Rnd 2: (Work FPhdc around next st, work BPhdc around next st) around.

Rnd 3: ★ Work FPhdc around next st, work BPhdc around next st; repeat from ★ 18 times **more**, work FPsc around next st, work BPsc around next st.

Rnd 4: Sc in Front Loop Only of each st around.

The free loops of Rnd 3 are available to be used if you have decided to line the Mitts.

Leaving a very short end, **loosely** lay second color on top of Rnd 4. Work over unused color throughout.

Beginning at Rnd 21, follow desired Chart.

Rnd 21: With color indicated on Chart and working in both loops, sc in next sc, remove marker and place **between** vertical posts of st just made **(now and throughout)**, sc in each sc around.

Rnds 22-29: Work split sc around.

Slip loop from hook onto marker; do **not** cut either yarn. Upper Hand complete.

THUMB JOINING
With **right** sides together, place Thumb and Upper Hand with the stitches to be joined together. Remove loop from Thumb marker and place on hook. Working from **wrong** side of Upper Hand, insert hook through st on Upper Hand and through st on Thumb *(Fig. 7, page 22)*, YO **tightly** and draw through sts and loop on hook, ch 1 **tightly**, finish off.

Do **not** pull tightly on either strand of Thumb yarn or a tight "band" will form around the Thumb. The Thumb and the Upper Hand are joined into one piece.

LOWER HAND
 MITT WITHOUT CUFF START HERE
Rnds 30-61: Work same as Rnds 30-61 of Mitten Without Cuff, page 24.

If you have decided not to line the Mitts, block them *(see Blocking, page 62)*.

If you have decided to line the Mitts, block them first *(see Blocking, page 62)*; then see "Lumpy & Bumpy" Lining, page 34 or "Smooth" Lining, page 35.

 **MITT WITH CUFF START HERE**

Rnds 30-48: Work same as Rnds 30-48 of Mitten With Cuff, page 22: 40 split sc.

Work even around until you reach the round marked "Stop for Cuff."

CUFF

Making sure loop on the hook is same color as Thumb Ribbing, cut unused color leaving a 3" (7.5 cm) end.

Rnd 1: Work split sc in next split sc, move marker to Back Loop Only of st just made, working over yarn end, work split sc around.

Rnd 2: Working in Front Loops Only, sc in first split sc, leaving first marker in Back Loop Only for lining placement, place second marker to indicate beginning of rnd, sc in each split sc around.

The free loops of Rnd 1 are available to be used if you have decided to line the Mitts.

Rnd 3: Work FPsc around next sc, work BPsc around next sc, (work FPhdc around next sc, work BPhdc around next sc) around.

Rnd 4: (Work FPhdc around next st, work BPhdc around next st) around.

Repeat Rnd 4 for pattern until Cuff is desired length.

Last Rnd: ★ Work FPhdc around next st, work BPhdc around next st; repeat from ★ 18 times **more**, work FPsc around next st, work BPsc around next st; slip st in next st, finish off.

If you have decided not to line the Mitts, block them *(see Blocking, page 62)*.

If you have decided to line the Mitts, block them first *(see Blocking, page 62)*; then see "Lumpy & Bumpy" Lining, page 34 or "Smooth" Lining, page 35.

Fingerless Mitt Linings

 EASY +

"The Linings are essentially slightly smaller mitts that are attached to the bottoms of outer mitts that have been made a little bigger than the perfect fit. For best results, use a soft yarn that is a lighter weight than what you used for the outer mitt. If you do use yarn that is of the exact same weight as the outer mitt, use a smaller size hook than what you used for the outer mitt. Be sure to block your Mitts first (see Blocking, page 62)."

> You will need
> 3 split-ring markers for either of these linings.

"LUMPY & BUMPY"

MITT WITH CUFF START HERE

Work same as Mitten With Cuff "Lumpy & Bumpy" Lining on page 27 through Rnd 4 of Upper Hand, page 28; do **not** finish off, drop loop from hook and place onto marker: 37 sts.

Flipping Upper Hand Ribbing down, push Lining inside the Mitt. Place loop back onto hook.

Joining Rnd: With Lining facing, working in Back Loop Only of each st around Lining **and** in free loops on Rnd 3 of Upper Hand Ribbing, sc in next st, (sc in next st on Mitt **only**, sc in next 12 sts) 3 times; slip st in next st, finish off.

THUMB LINING

Turn the Mitt completely inside out with the Lining on the outside. This will be a little awkward since the outside of the Mitt is larger than the Lining, but the Lining is stretchy so it works out fine. It helps if you push the Mitt Thumb down a little so the Lining relaxes enough to allow you to work the next round.

Rnd 1: Leaving a 3" (7.5 cm) end and with inside of Lining facing, insert hook through **both** marked sts, remove marker, YO and pull up a loop, ch 1, sc in same st, place marker in sc just made to indicate the beginning of rnd, working over yarn end, hdc in each st around, drop loop from hook and place onto marker: 15 sts.

Push the Mitt Thumb inside of the Lining Thumb. Place loop back onto hook.

Joining Rnd: With Lining facing, working in Back Loop Only of each st around Lining **and** in free loops on Rnd 2 of Thumb Ribbing, sc in next st, sc in next st on Mitt **only**, sc in next 12 sts; slip st in next sc, finish off.

MITT WITHOUT CUFF START HERE

Work same as Mitten Without Cuff "Lumpy & Bumpy" Lining on page 27 through Rnd 4 of Upper Hand, page 28; do **not** finish off, drop loop from hook and place onto marker: 37 sts.

Flipping Upper Hand Ribbing down, push Lining inside the Mitt. Place loop back onto hook.

Joining Rnd: With Lining facing, working in Back Loop Only of each st around Lining **and** in free loops on Rnd 3 of Upper Hand Ribbing, sc in next st, (sc in next st on Mitt **only**, sc in next 12 sts) 3 times; slip st in next st, finish off.

THUMB LINING
Work same as Mitt With Cuff.

"SMOOTH"

MITT WITH CUFF START HERE

Work same as Mitten With Cuff "Smooth" Lining on page 27 through Rnd 7 of Upper Hand, page 28; do **not** finish off, drop loop from hook and place onto marker: 37 sc.

Flipping Upper Hand Ribbing down, push Lining inside the Mitt. Place loop back onto hook.

Joining Rnd: With Lining facing, working in Back Loop Only of each st around Lining **and** in free loops on Rnd 3 of Upper Hand Ribbing, sc through **both** layers of next st, (sc in next st on Mitt **only**, sc through **both** layers of next 12 sts) 3 times; slip st in next st, finish off.

THUMB LINING
Turn the Mitt completely inside out with the Lining on the outside. This will be a little awkward since the outside of the Mitt is larger than the Lining, but the Lining is stretchy so it works out fine. It helps if you push the Mitt Thumb down a little so the Lining relaxes enough to allow you to work the next round.

Rnd 1: Leaving a 3" (7.5 cm) end and with inside of Lining facing, insert hook through **both** marked sts, remove marker, YO and pull up a loop, ch 1, sc in same st, place marker in sc just made to indicate the beginning of rnd, working over yarn end, hdc in each st around, drop loop from hook and place onto marker: 15 sts.

Push the Mitt Thumb inside of the Lining Thumb. Place loop back onto hook.

Joining Rnd: With Lining facing, working in Back Loop Only of each st around Lining **and** in free loops on Rnd 2 of Thumb Ribbing, sc in next st, sc in next st on Mitt **only**, sc in next 12 sts; slip st in next sc, finish off.

MITT WITHOUT CUFF START HERE

Work same as Mitten Without Cuff "Smooth" Lining on page 27 through Rnd 7 of Upper Hand, page 28; do **not** finish off, drop loop from hook and place onto marker: 37 sc.

Flipping Upper Hand Ribbing down, push Lining inside the Mitt. Place loop back onto hook.

Joining Rnd: With Lining facing, working in Back Loop Only of each st around Lining **and** in free loops on Rnd 3 of Upper Hand Ribbing, sc in next st, (sc in next st on Mitt **only**, sc in next 12 sts) 3 times; slip st in next st, finish off.

THUMB LINING
Work same as Mitt With Cuff.

Texting Mitten with Cuff

"It's very important that you follow the instructions closely to be sure you make one right-handed and one left-handed texting mitten. They are not the same!"

Follow Charts throughout (*see Following a Chart, page 62 and Changing Colors, page 63*).

You will need 3 split-ring markers, 4 buttons, sewing needle and matching thread for this version.

STITCH GUIDE

SPLIT SINGLE CROCHET
(abbreviated split sc)
Insert hook **between** vertical posts of next st and **under** unused strand on previous rnd, YO and pull up a loop slightly higher than loop on hook using a pivoting motion while keeping first loop snug on the hook, YO and draw through both loops on hook **(split sc completed; *Figs. 1-6, page 16*).**

SLIP STITCH 2 TOGETHER
(abbreviated slip st2tog)
(uses next 2 sts)
Insert hook in Front Loop Only of next 2 sts *(Fig. 14, page 63)*, YO and draw though loop on hook.

INCREASE (uses one st)
Sc in next st, work split sc **between** vertical posts of **same** st.

FRONT POST HALF DOUBLE CROCHET
(abbreviated FPhdc)
YO, insert hook from **front** to **back** around post of st indicated *(Fig. 17, page 63)*, YO and pull up a loop, YO and draw through all 3 loops on hook.

BACK POST HALF DOUBLE CROCHET
(abbreviated BPhdc)
YO, insert hook from **back** to **front** around post of st indicated *(Fig. 17, page 63)*, YO and pull up a loop, YO and draw through all 3 loops on hook.

FRONT POST SINGLE CROCHET
(abbreviated FPsc)
Insert hook from **front** to **back** around post of st indicated *(Fig. 17, page 63)*, YO and pull up a loop, YO and draw through both loops on hook.

BACK POST SINGLE CROCHET
(abbreviated BPsc)
Insert hook from **back** to **front** around post of st indicated *(Fig. 17, page 63)*, YO and pull up a loop, YO and draw through both loops on hook.

"The first rounds are difficult because they are small, the increases make the unused strand pull down out of sight and the color changes are awkward. Try to remain relaxed. If you get uptight and frustrated, your stitches will be too tight. Set your work down once in a while. It won't fall apart and you'll soon start to realize that you don't need to grip it to keep it intact. Relax and take one stitch at a time. If you are struggling to get the hook into each stitch, you are working too tightly. You will need to loosen your tension or use a larger size hook."

RIGHT TEXTING MITTEN THUMB

With first color indicated on desired Chart, ch 3 **tightly**, place marker around ch-3; join with slip st to form a ring with marker in center.

Rnd 1 (Right side): Ch 1, sc **loosely** in ring, remove marker and place **between** vertical posts of sc just made to mark first sp **and** the beginning of rnd *(see Markers, page 62)*, pull yarn end to back of work, work 7 sc **loosely** in ring; do **not** join: 8 sc.

Leaving a very short end, **loosely** lay second color on top of Rnd 1. Work over unused color throughout.

Rnd 2: Work split sc in marked st, remove marker and place **between** vertical posts of st just made **(now and throughout)**, work split sc, increase twice, work 2 split sc, increase twice: 12 sts.

Rnd 3: Work 2 split sc, increase, work split sc, increase, work 3 split sc, (increase, work split sc) twice: 16 sts.

Rnds 4-9: Work split sc around.

Rnd 10 (Thumb opening)**:** Insert hook **between** vertical posts of next split sc, YO and pull up a loop, YO with **both** colors and draw through both loops on hook (one loop of **each** color on hook) **(counts as split sc, now and throughout)**, drop desired edging color loop from hook and place onto marker to keep it from unraveling **(Fig. 10a)**, with non-edging color ch 8; drop loop from hook and place onto another marker, remove marker from edging color loop and place onto hook, with ch-8 in **front** of work, work 6 split sc (do **not** work over ch) **(Fig. 10b)**, drop loop from hook and place onto marker, being careful **not** to twist ch, remove marker from non-edging color and place loop on hook, remove edging color loop from marker and place on hook (2 loops on hook) **(Fig. 10c)**, working **over** unused color, insert hook **between** vertical posts of next split sc, with color indicated, YO and pull up a loop, YO and draw through all 3 loops on hook **(counts as split sc, now and throughout)**, work 8 split sc.

Fig. 10a

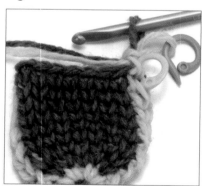

Fig. 10b

Fig. 10c

Rnd 11: Work split sc in next split sc changing to second color, skip next ch, sc in back ridge of next 7 chs **(Fig. 13, page 63)**, work 8 split sc: 16 sts.

Rnds 12 and 13: Work split sc around; at end of Rnd 13, complete last st by changing to same color as first st of rnd, remove marker. Drop loop from hook and place onto marker to keep piece from unraveling, cut same color leaving a 12" (30.5 cm) end and cut unused color leaving a 3" (7.5 cm) end. Set Thumb aside.

UPPER & LOWER HAND

Rnd 1 (Right side)**:** With first color indicated on desired Chart, ch 8 (button loop), work 4 sc in second ch from hook, place marker **between** vertical posts of first sc made, pull remaining chs and yarn end to **front** of work, work 4 more sc in same ch **(Fig. 11)**: 8 sc.

Fig. 11

Leaving a very short end, **loosely** lay second color on top of Rnd 1. Work over unused color throughout.

Rnd 2: Keeping chs and yarn end to **front** of work, work 2 split sc, increase twice, work 2 split sc, increase, sc in next st, insert hook through last ch of button loop and **between** vertical posts of same st as last sc, pull up a loop, YO and draw through both loops on hook: 12 sts.

Pull yarn end to back of work and secure.

Rnds 3-20: Work same as Mitten With Cuff, page 22: 40 split sc.

Rnd 21 (Hand opening): Insert hook **between** vertical posts of next split sc, YO and pull up a loop, YO with **both** colors and draw through both loops on hook (one loop of **each** color on hook), drop edging color loop from hook and place onto marker to keep piece from unraveling, with non-edging color ch 19, skip next 19 split sc, being careful **not** to twist ch, slip st in next split sc, drop loop from hook and place onto marker, remove marker from edging color loop and place onto hook, work 9 split sc, (slip st, ch 7, slip st) in next split sc (button loop), work 8 split sc, drop loop from hook and place onto marker, remove marker from non-edging color and place loop on hook, remove edging color loop from marker and place on hook (2 loops on hook), working **over** unused color, insert hook **between** vertical posts of next split sc, with color indicated, YO and pull up a loop, YO and draw through all 3 loops on hook, work 20 split sc.

Rnd 22: Work split sc in next split sc, sc in back ridge of next 19 chs, work 20 split sc: 40 sts.

Rnds 23-48: Work same as Mitten With Cuff, pages 22 and 23.

CUFF
Work same as Cuff, page 23.

LEFT TEXTING MITTEN
THUMB

Rnds 1-9: Work same as Right Texting Mitten Thumb on page 37: 16 sts.

Rnd 10 (Thumb opening)**:** Work 8 split sc, insert hook **between** vertical posts of next split sc, YO and pull up a loop, YO with **both** colors and draw through both loops on hook (one loop of **each** color on hook), drop edging color loop from hook and place onto marker to keep it from unraveling, with non-edging color ch 8; drop loop from hook and place onto another marker, remove marker from edging color loop, with ch-8 in **front** of work, work 6 split sc (do **not** work over ch), drop loop from hook and place onto marker, being careful **not** to twist ch, remove marker from non-edging color and place loop on hook, remove edging color loop from marker and place on hook (2 loops on hook), working **over** unused color, insert hook **between** vertical posts of next split sc, with color indicated, YO and pull up a loop, YO and draw through all 3 loops on hook.

Rnd 11: Work 9 split sc, skip next ch, sc in back ridge of next 7 chs: 16 sts.

Rnds 12 and 13: Work split sc around; at end of Rnd 13, complete last st by changing to same color as first st of rnd, remove marker. Drop loop from hook and place onto marker to keep piece from unraveling, cut same color leaving a 12" (30.5 cm) end and cut unused color leaving a 3" (7.5 cm) end. Set Thumb aside.

UPPER & LOWER HAND

Rnds 1-20: Work same as Right Upper & Lower Hand on page 38: 40 split sc.

Rnd 21: Work 20 split sc, insert hook **between** vertical posts of next split sc, YO and pull up a loop, YO with **both** colors and draw through both loops on hook (2 loops on hook), drop edging color loop from hook and place onto marker to keep it from unraveling, with non-edging color ch 19, skip next 19 split sc, being careful **not** to twist ch, slip st in next split sc, drop loop from hook and place onto marker, remove marker from edging color and place on hook, skip next split sc, work 9 split sc, (slip st, ch 7, slip st) in next split sc (button loop), work 8 split sc, drop edging color loop from hook and place onto marker, remove marker from non-edging color and place loop onto hook, remove edging color loop from marker and place on hook (2 loops on hook), working **over** unused color, insert hook **between** vertical posts of next split sc, with color indicated, YO and pull up a loop, YO and draw through all 3 loops on hook.

Rnd 22: Work 21 split sc, sc in back ridge of next 19 chs: 40 sts.

Rnds 23-48: Work same as Mitten With Cuff, pages 22 and 23.

CUFF

Work same as Cuff, page 23.

If you have decided to not line the Mittens, block them *(see Blocking, page 62)*. After blocking, sew one button to the palm and one button to the back of the hand to hold texting flaps in place on each Mitten.

If you have decided to line the Mittens, block them first *(see Blocking, page 62)*; then see "Lumpy & Bumpy" Lining, page 44 or "Smooth" Lining, page 46.

Texting Mitten without Cuff

"It's very important that you follow the instructions closely to be sure you make one right-handed and one left-handed texting mitten. They are not the same!"

EASY +

Follow Charts throughout *(see Following a Chart, page 62 and Changing Colors, page 63)*.

STITCH GUIDE

SLIP STITCH 2 TOGETHER
(abbreviated slip st2tog)
(uses next 2 split sc)
Insert hook in Front Loop Only of next 2 split sc *(Fig. 14, page 63)*, YO and draw though sts **and** loop on hook.

> You will need 3 split-ring markers, 4 buttons, sewing needle and matching thread for this version.

RIGHT TEXTING MITTEN
THUMB

Following desired Chart, work same as Right Texting Mitten With Cuff, page 37.

UPPER & LOWER HAND

Rnds 1-48: Work same as Right Texting Mitten With Cuff on pages 38 and 39; do **not** finish off: 40 split sc.

Rnds 49-59: Work split sc around.

Rnd 60: Cut unused color leaving 3" (7.5 cm) end, work split sc in next st, place marker in Front Loop Only of st just made *(Fig. 14, page 63)*, working over yarn end, work split sc around.

Reverse direction by turning your work counterclockwise so you are working from the inside of the Mitten. This will feel awkward, but don't worry, it will look fine. Reversing direction ensures that the stitches in the next round will curl slightly toward the inside of the Mitten for a nice finish.

Rnd 61: Turn; skip next st, working in Front Loops Only, slip st in next st, place marker in st just made, (slip st in next 17 sts, slip st2tog) twice, slip st in same st as marker, do **not** remove marker if planning on lining Mittens, finish off: 37 sts.

LEFT TEXTING MITTEN
THUMB

Following desired Chart, work same as Left Texting Mitten With Cuff, page 40.

UPPER & LOWER HAND

Rnds 1-48: Work same as Left Texting Mitten With Cuff, page 40: 40 split sc.

Rnds 49-61: Work same as Right Texting Mitten Without Cuff, page 42.

If you have decided not to line the Mittens, block them *(see Blocking, page 62)*. After blocking, sew one button to the palm and one button to the back of the hand to hold texting flaps in place on each Mitten.

The free loops of Rnd 60 are available to be used if you have decided to line the Mittens. Block them first *(see Blocking, page 62)*; then see "Lumpy & Bumpy" Lining, page 44 or "Smooth" Lining, page 46.

"LUMPY & BUMPY"

"The linings are essentially slightly smaller mittens that are attached to the bottoms of outer mittens that have been made a little bigger than the perfect fit. For best results, use a soft yarn that is a lighter weight than what you used for the outer mittens. If you do use yarn that is of the exact same weight as the outer mitten, be sure to use a smaller size hook than what you used for the outer mitten. Be sure to block your Mittens first (see Blocking, page 62)."

 ### RIGHT MITTEN WITH CUFF START HERE

Work same as Mitten With Cuff "Lumpy & Bumpy" Lining on page 27 through Rnd 4 of Upper Hand, page 28; do **not** finish off: 37 sts.

Rnd 5 (Joining rnd): Sc in next tr, (tr in next sc, sc in next tr) 9 times, slip loop from hook and place onto marker, turn the Mitten completely inside out with the Lining on the outside, remove loop from marker and place on hook, with Lining facing you, working through free loops of chs *(Fig. 15b, page 63)* across bottom of opening (Rnd 21) **and** in sts on Rnd 4 of Lining, skip first ch, sc in next 18 sts.

Rnd 6 (Joining rnd): Tr in next sc, (sc in next tr, tr in next sc) 9 times; working in Front Loops Only of split sc across top of opening (Rnd 21) **and** in sts on Rnd 5 of Lining, (sc in next st, tr in next st) 9 times.

Rnd 7: Sc in next tr, (tr in next sc, sc in next tr) around.

Rnd 8: Tr in next sc, (sc in next tr, tr in next sc) around.

Rnds 9 and 10: Repeat Rnds 7 and 8.

SHAPING
Complete same as "Lumpy & Bumpy" Lining, page 28.

THUMB LINING
Push the Mitten Thumb down a little so the Lining relaxes enough to allow you to work the next round.

Rnd 1: Leaving a 3" (7.5 cm) end and inside of Lining facing, insert hook through **both** marked sts, remove marker, YO and pull up a loop, ch 1, sc in same st, place marker in sc just made to indicate beginning of the rnd, working over yarn end, hdc in each st around, drop loop from hook and place onto marker: 15 sts.

Rnd 2: Hdc in next 9 hdc, working in free loops of chs across bottom of opening (Rnd 10) **and** in sts on Rnd 1 of Lining, skip first ch, sc in next 6 sts.

Rnd 3: Hdc in next 8 hdc; working in Front Loops Only of split sc across top of opening (Rnd 10) **and** in sts on Rnd 2 of Lining, sc in next 7 sts.

Rnds 4 and 5: Hdc in each st around.

Rnd 6: Hdc2tog, hdc in next 3 hdc, hdc2tog twice, hdc in next 4 hdc, hdc2tog: 11 hdc.

Rnd 7: Hdc2tog, hdc in next hdc, hdc2tog twice, hdc in next 2 hdc, hdc2tog: 7 hdc.

Closing: Fold last rnd flat with yarn at side edge, remove marker, working through **both** layers, slip st across, cut yarn leaving 3" (7.5 cm) end; finish off, pull yarn end to inside of lining, out of sight. Thumb Lining complete.

 LEFT MITTEN WITH CUFF START HERE
Work same as Mitten With Cuff "Lumpy & Bumpy" Lining on page 27 through Rnd 4 of Upper Hand, page 28; do **not** finish off: 37 sts.

Rnd 5 (Joining rnd): Slip loop from hook and place onto marker, turn the Mitten completely inside out with the Lining on the outside, remove loop from marker and place on hook, with Lining facing you, working through free loops of chs across bottom of opening (Rnd 21) **and** in sts on Rnd 4 of Lining, skip first ch, sc in next 18 sts, sc in next tr, (tr in next sc, sc in next tr) 9 times.

Rnd 6 (Joining rnd): Working in Front Loops Only of split sc across top of opening (Rnd 21) **and** in sts on Rnd 5 of Lining, (sc in next st, tr in next st) 9 times, tr in next sc, (sc in next tr, tr in next sc) 9 times.

Complete same as Right Mitten With Cuff, page 44.

Sew one button to the palm and one button to the back of the hand to hold texting flaps in place on each Mitten.

 RIGHT MITTEN WITHOUT CUFF START HERE
Work same as Mitten Without Cuff "Lumpy & Bumpy" Lining on page 27 through Rnd 4 of Upper Hand, page 28; do **not** finish off: 37 sts.

Rnd 5 (Joining rnd): Sc in next tr, (tr in next sc, sc in next tr) 9 times, drop loop from hook and place onto marker, turn the Mitten completely inside out with the Lining on the outside, remove loop from marker and place onto hook, with Lining facing you, working through free loops of chs *(Fig. 15b, page 63)* across bottom of opening (Rnd 21) **and** in sts on Rnd 4 of Lining, skip first ch, sc in next 18 sts.

Rnd 6 (Joining rnd)**:** Tr in next sc, (sc in next tr, tr in next sc) 9 times; working in Front Loops Only of split sc across top of opening (Rnd 21) **and** in sts on Rnd 5 of Lining, (sc in next st, tr in next st) 9 times.

Complete same as Right Mitten With Cuff, page 45.

LEFT MITTEN WITHOUT CUFF START HERE

Work same as Mitten Without Cuff "Lumpy & Bumpy" Lining on page 27 through Rnd 4 of Upper Hand, page 28; do **not** finish off: 37 sts.

Rnd 5 (Joining rnd)**:** Drop loop from hook and place onto marker, turn the Mitten completely inside out with the Lining on the outside, remove loop from marker and place onto hook, with Lining facing you, working through free loops of chs across bottom of opening (Rnd 21) **and** in sts on Rnd 4 of

Lining, skip first ch, sc in next 18 sts, sc in next tr, (tr in next sc, sc in next tr) 9 times.

Rnd 6 (Joining rnd)**:** Working in Front Loops Only of split sc across top of opening (Rnd 21) **and** in sts on Rnd 5 of Lining, (sc in next st, tr in next st) 9 times, tr in next sc, (sc in next tr, tr in next sc) 9 times.

Complete same as Right Mitten With Cuff, page 45.

Sew one button to the palm and one button to the back of the hand to hold texting flaps in place on each Mitten.

"SMOOTH"

RIGHT MITTEN WITH CUFF START HERE

Work same as Mitten With Cuff "Smooth" Lining on page 28 through Rnd 4 of Upper Hand, page 29; do **not** finish off: 37 sts.

Rnd 5 (Joining rnd)**:** Sc in next 19 sc, drop loop from hook and place onto marker, turn the Mitten completely inside out with the Lining on the outside, remove loop from marker and place onto hook, with Lining facing you, working through free loops of chs *(Fig. 15b, page 63)* across bottom of opening (Rnd 21) **and** in sts on Rnd 4 of Lining, skip first ch, sc in next 18 sts.

Rnd 6 (Joining rnd)**:** Sc in next 19 sc, working in Front Loops Only of split sc across top of opening (Rnd 21) **and** in sts on Rnd 5 of Lining, sc in next 18 sts.

Complete same as Mitten With Cuff "Smooth" Lining on page 29.

THUMB LINING

Work same as Thumb Lining on page 45.

 LEFT MITTEN WITH CUFF START HERE

Work same as Mitten With Cuff "Smooth" Lining on page 28 through Rnd 4 of Upper Hand, page 29; do **not** finish off: 37 sts.

Rnd 5 (Joining rnd): Drop loop from hook and place onto marker, turn the Mitten completely inside out with the Lining on the outside, remove loop from marker and place on hook, with Lining facing you, working through free loops of chs across bottom of opening (Rnd 21) **and** in sts on Rnd 5 of Lining, skip first ch, sc in next 18 sts, sc in next 19 sc on Lining Only.

Rnd 6 (Joining rnd): Working in Front Loops Only of split sc across top of opening (Rnd 21) **and** in sts on Rnd 5 of Lining, sc in next 18 sts, sc in next 19 sc on Lining Only.

Complete same as Right Mitten.

Sew one button to the palm and one button to the back of the hand to hold texting flaps in place on each Mitten.

 RIGHT MITTEN WITHOUT CUFF START HERE

Work same as Mitten Without Cuff "Smooth" Lining on page 29 through Rnd 4 of Upper Hand; do **not** finish off: 37 sts.

Rnd 5 (Joining rnd)**:** Sc in next 19 sc, drop loop from hook and place onto marker, turn the Mitten completely inside out with the Lining on the outside, remove loop from marker and place onto hook, with Lining facing you, working through free loops of chs (**Fig. 15b, page 63**) across bottom of opening (Rnd 21) **and** in sts on Rnd 4 of Lining, skip first ch, sc in next 18 sts.

Rnd 6 (Joining rnd)**:** Sc in next 19 sc, working in Front Loops Only of split sc across top of opening (Rnd 21) **and** in sts on Rnd 5 of Lining, sc in next 18 sts.

Complete same as Mitten With Cuff "Smooth" Lining on page 29.

THUMB LINING

Work same as Thumb Lining on page 45.

 LEFT MITTEN WITHOUT CUFF START HERE

Work same as Mitten Without Cuff "Smooth" Lining on page 28 through Rnd 4 of Upper Hand, page 29; do **not** finish off: 37 sts.

Rnd 5 (Joining rnd): Drop loop from hook and place onto marker, turn the Mitten completely inside out with the Lining on the outside, remove loop from marker and place onto hook, with Lining facing you, working through free loops of chs across bottom of opening (Rnd 21) **and** in sts on Rnd 4 of Lining, skip first ch, sc in next 18 sts, sc in next 19 sc on Lining Only.

Rnd 6 (Joining rnd)**:** Working in Front Loops Only of split sc across top of opening (Rnd 21) **and** in sts on Rnd 5 of Lining, sc in next 18 sts, sc in next 19 sc on Lining Only.

Complete same as Right Mitten.

THUMB LINING

Work same as Thumb Lining on page 45.

Sew one button to the palm and one button to the back of the hand to hold texting flaps in place on each Mitten.

ARGYLE

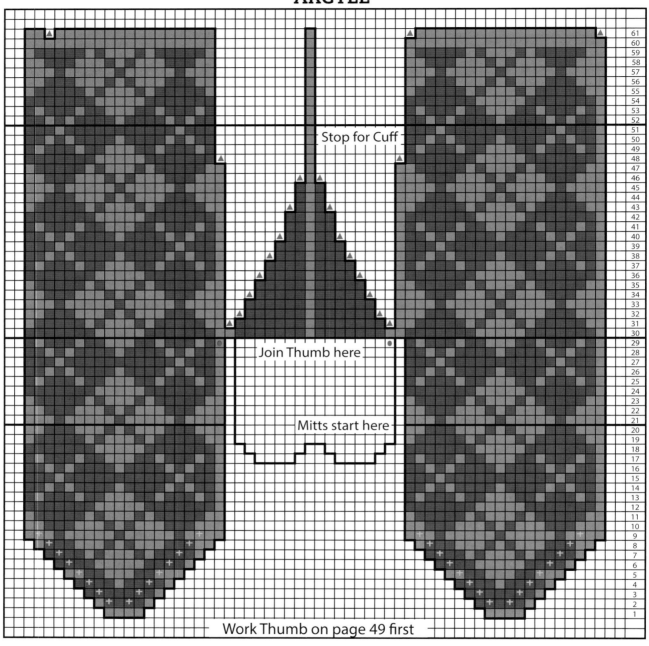

Stop for Cuff

Join Thumb here

Mitts start here

Work Thumb on page 49 first

61	
60	
59	
58	
57	
56	
55	
54	
53	
52	
51	
50	
49	
48	
47	
46	
45	
44	
43	
42	
41	
40	
39	
38	
37	
36	
35	
34	
33	
32	
31	
30	
29	
28	
27	
26	
25	
24	
23	
22	
21	
20	
19	
18	
17	
16	
15	
14	
13	
12	
11	
10	
9	
8	
7	
6	
5	
4	
3	
2	
1	

KEY

■ - MC   ● - Join

■ - CC   ▲ - Decrease

+ - Increase

3-COLOR ARGYLE

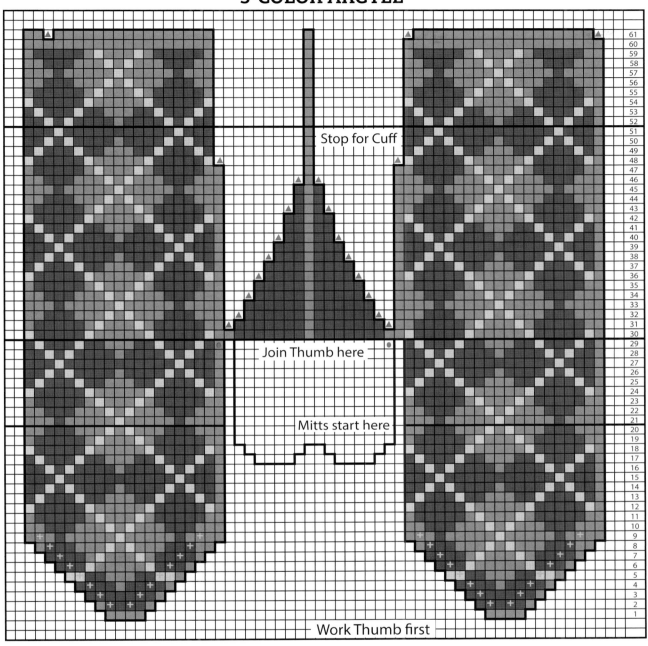

Stop for Cuff

Join Thumb here

Mitts start here

Work Thumb first

61
60
59
58
57
56
55
54
53
52
51
50
49
48
47
46
45
44
43
42
41
40
39
38
37
36
35
34
33
32
31
30
29
28
27
26
25
24
23
22
21
20
19
18
17
16
15
14
13
12
11
10
9
8
7
6
5
4
3
2
1

KEY

 - MC

█ - CC1

░ - CC2

✛ - Increase

● - Join

▲ - Decrease

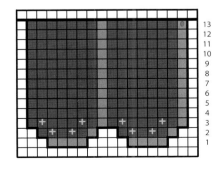

13
12
11
10
9
8
7
6
5
4
3
2
1

DIAMONDS

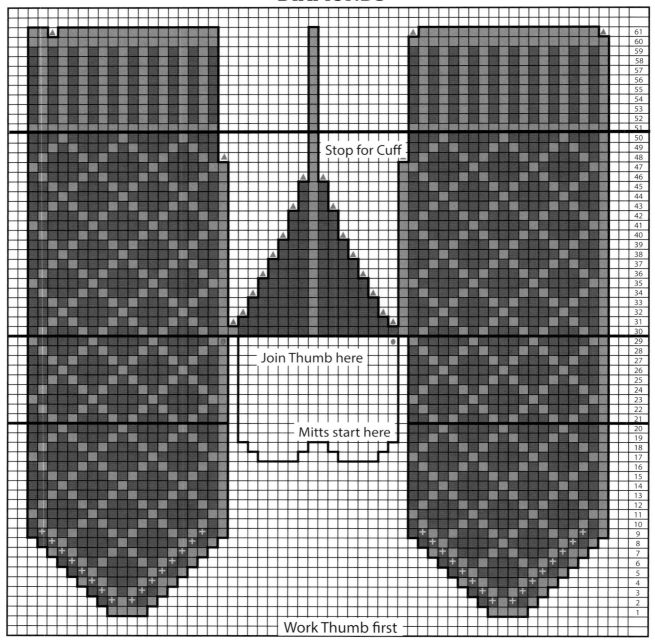

Stop for Cuff

Join Thumb here

Mitts start here

Work Thumb first

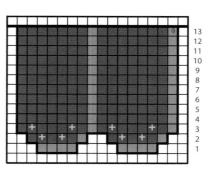

FISH SKELETON

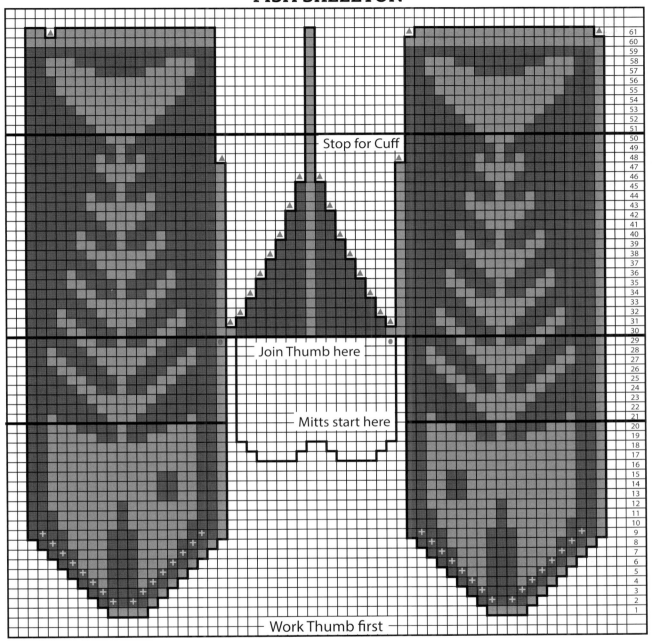

Stop for Cuff

Join Thumb here

Mitts start here

Work Thumb first

Row
61
60
59
58
57
56
55
54
53
52
51
50
49
48
47
46
45
44
43
42
41
40
39
38
37
36
35
34
33
32
31
30
29
28
27
26
25
24
23
22
21
20
19
18
17
16
15
14
13
12
11
10
9
8
7
6
5
4
3
2
1

KEY

 - MC

- CC

+ - Increase

• - Join

▲ - Decrease

Row
13
12
11
10
9
8
7
6
5
4
3
2
1

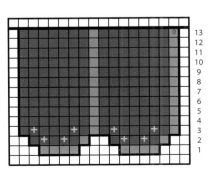

51

HEARTS

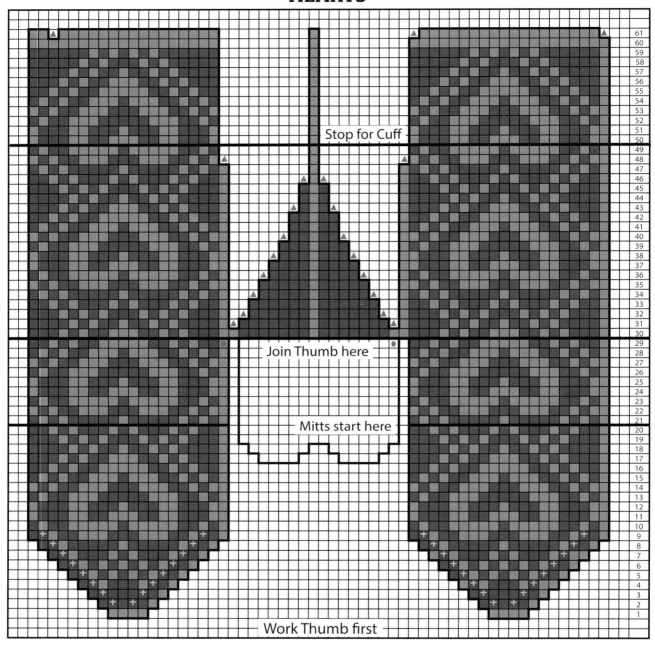

Stop for Cuff

Join Thumb here

Mitts start here

Work Thumb first

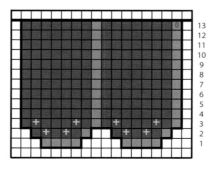

HOUNDSTOOTH

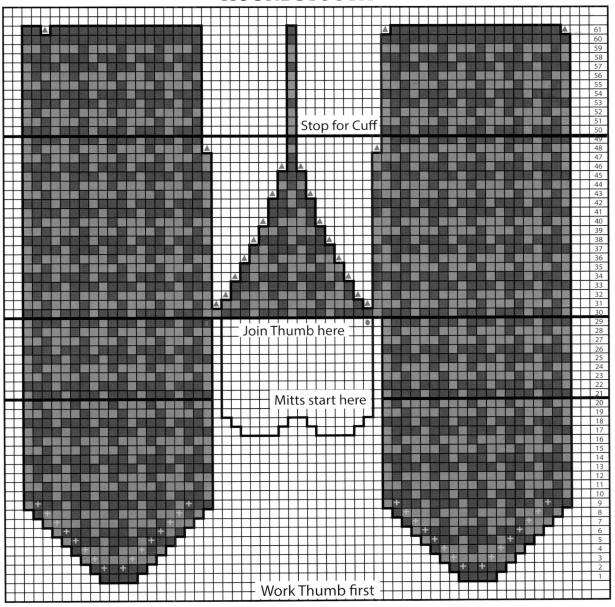

Stop for Cuff

Join Thumb here

Mitts start here

Work Thumb first

KEY

 - MC

- CC

+ - Increase

● - Join

▲ - Decrease

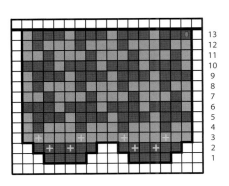

HUGS & KISSES

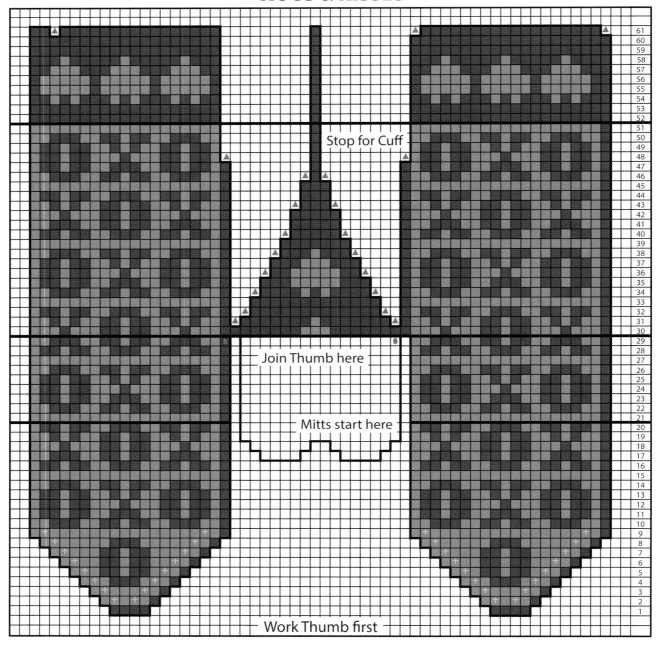

Stop for Cuff

Join Thumb here

Mitts start here

Work Thumb first

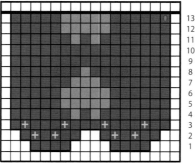

PLAID

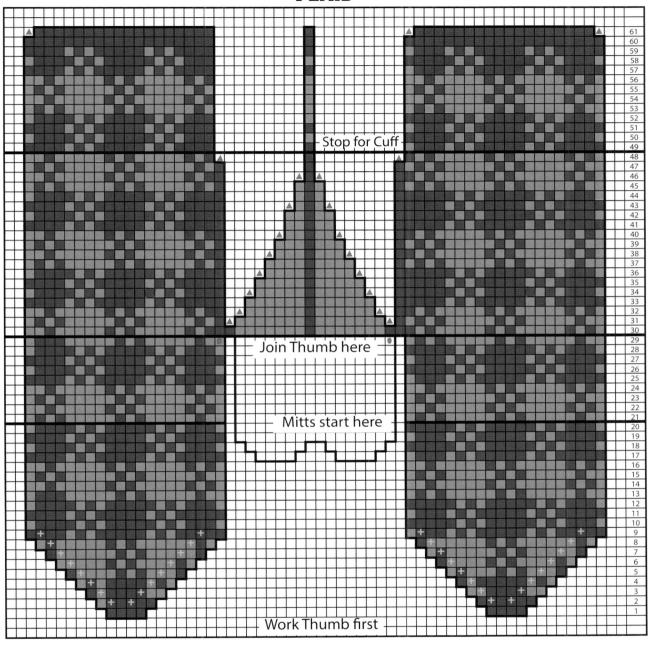

Stop for Cuff

Join Thumb here

Mitts start here

Work Thumb first

61	60	59	58	57	56	55

KEY

- ■ – MC
- ▨ – CC
- + – Increase
- ● – Join
- ▲ – Decrease

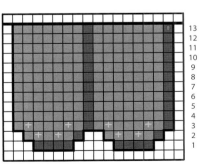

SIMPLE DOTS

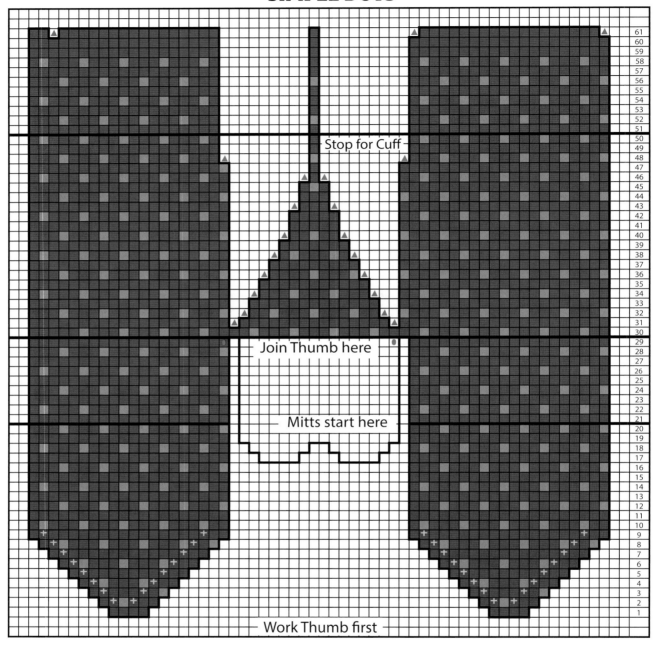

Stop for Cuff

Join Thumb here

Mitts start here

Work Thumb first

61 60 59 58 57 56 55 54 53 52 51 50 49 48 47 46 45 44 43 42 41 40 39 38 37 36 35 34 33 32 31 30 29 28 27 26 25 24 23 22 21 20 19 18 17 16 15 14 13 12 11 10 9 8 7 6 5 4 3 2 1

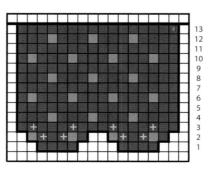

13 12 11 10 9 8 7 6 5 4 3 2 1

SNOWFLAKES

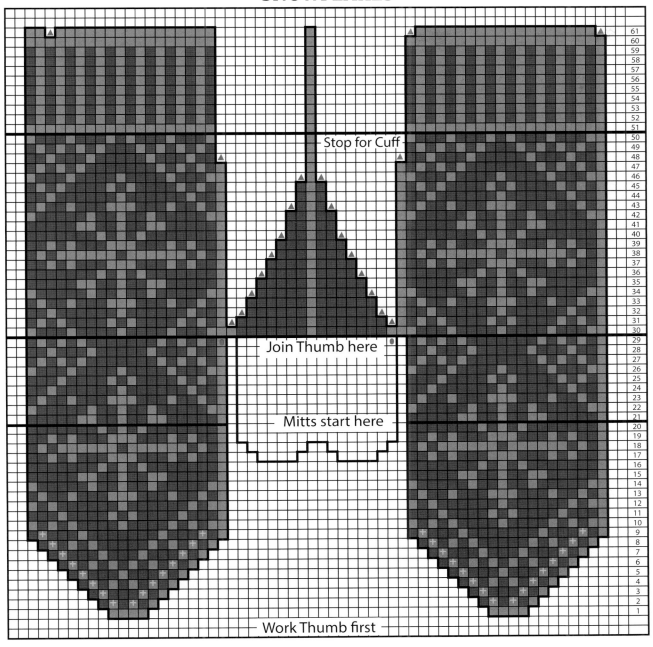

Stop for Cuff

Join Thumb here

Mitts start here

Work Thumb first

KEY

- ◼ - MC
- ◼ - CC
- + - Increase
- ● - Join
- ▲ - Decrease

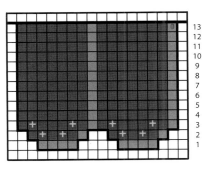

STARS & STRIPES - RIGHT HAND

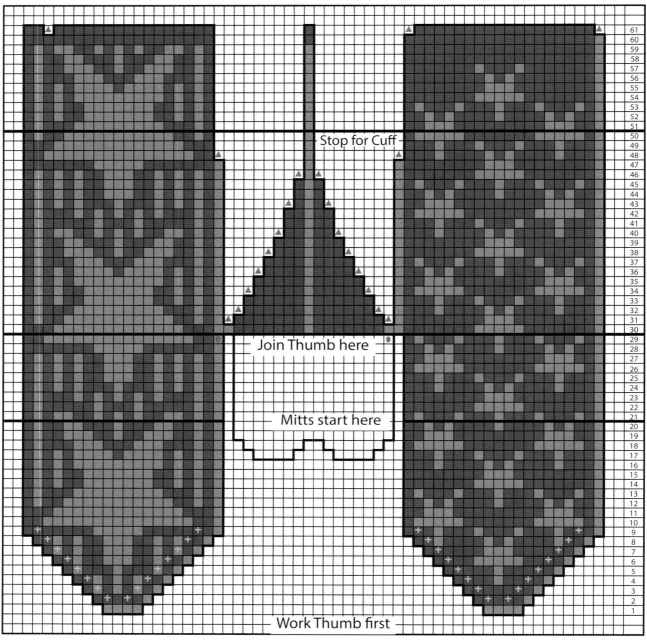

Stop for Cuff

Join Thumb here

Mitts start here

Work Thumb first

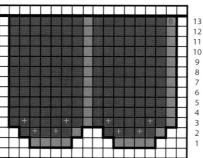

Note: Models shown were crocheted holding 2 strands of yarn together throughout, one strand **each** of Red and Blue for MC and 2 strands of White for CC. See Yarn Information, page 60.

STARS & STRIPES - LEFT HAND

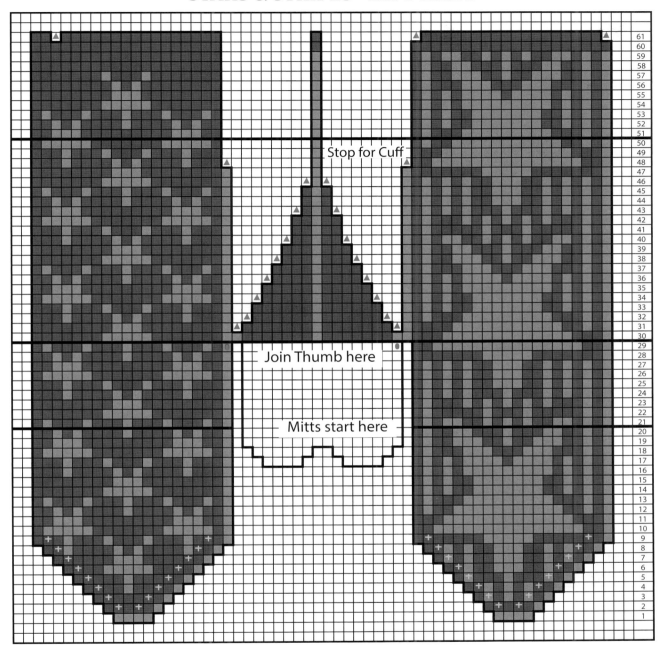

Stop for Cuff

Join Thumb here

Mitts start here

	61
	60
	59
	58
	57
	56
	55
	54
	53
	52
	51
	50
	49
	48
	47
	46
	45
	44
	43
	42
	41
	40
	39
	38
	37
	36
	35
	34
	33
	32
	31
	30
	29
	28
	27
	26
	25
	24
	23
	22
	21
	20
	19
	18
	17
	16
	15
	14
	13
	12
	11
	10
	9
	8
	7
	6
	5
	4
	3
	2
	1

KEY

■ - MC   ● - Join

■ - CC   ▲ - Decrease

✛ - Increase

Yarn Information

The Mittens in this book were made using a variety of yarns. Any brand of the specific weight of yarn may be used. It is best to refer to the yardage/meters when determining how many balls or skeins to purchase. Remember, to achieve the same look, it is the weight of yarn that is important, not the brand of yarn.

For your convenience, listed below are the specific yarns used to create our photography models. Because yarn manufacturers make frequent changes to their product lines, you may sometimes find it necessary to use a substitute yarn or to search for the discontinued product at alternate suppliers (locally or online).

ARGYLE - SMALL
Red Heart® Heart & Sole®
MC - #3540 Purple
CC - #3900 Fuchsia
Lining - #3930 Jellybeans

ARGYLE - MEDIUM
Lion Brand® LB Collection® Superwash Merino
MC - #145 Eggplant
CC - #194 Acid Green

ARGYLE - X-LARGE
Lion Brand® Wool-Ease®
MC - #153 Black
CC - #151 Gray Heather
Lion Brand® LB Collection® Baby Alpaca
Lining - #152 Silver Gray Heather

3-COLOR ARGYLE
Patons® Kroy Socks
MC - #55042 Gentry Gray
CC1 - #55045 Gray Marl
CC2 & Lining - #55705 Red

DIAMONDS
Patons® Kroy Socks FX
MC - #57330 Celestial Color
Patons® Kroy Socks
CC - #55045 Gray Marl
Red Heart® Heart & Sole®
Lining - #3540 Purple

FISH SKELETON
Premier Yarns® Serenity Sock™
MC - #150-09 Sky Blue
CC - #150-08 Hot Lime
Lining - #155-06 Dark Water

HEARTS
Patons® Classic Wool Dk Superwash™
MC - #12532 Claret
CC - #12008 Aran
Patons® Kroy Socks
Lining - #55714 Dad's Jacquard

HOUNDSTOOTH MITTS
Lion Brand® LB Collection® Superwash Merino
MC - #170 Dijon
CC - #098 Antique

HOUNDSTOOTH
Lion Brand® Vanna's Style
MC - #150 Charcoal
CC - #098 Ecru
Red Heart® Heart & Sole®
Lining - #3900 Fuchsia

HUGS & KISSES
Red Heart® Heart & Sole®
MC - #3540 Purple
CC - #3900 Fuchsia
Lining - #3934 Sorbeto

PLAID
Red Heart® Chic Sheep
MC - #5641 Sterling
CC - #5687 VIP
Lion Brand® LB Collection® Baby Alpaca
Lining - #152 Silver Gray Heather

SIMPLE DOTS
Patons® Kroy Socks
MC - #55011 Flax
CC - #55705 Red
Lining - #55048 Gray Brown Marl

SNOWFLAKES
Lion Brand® LB Collection® Superwash Merino
MC - #107 Sky
CC - #098 Antique
Lion Brand® LB Collection® Baby Alpaca
Lining - #098 Natural

STARS & STRIPES
Premier Yarns® Serenity Sock™
MC Red - #150-03 Red
MC Blue - #150-10 Navy
CC - #150-01 Soft White
Patons® Kroy Socks FX
Lining - #57110 Cadet Colors

General Instructions

ABBREVIATIONS

BPhdc	Back Post half double crochet(s)
BPsc	Back Post single crochet(s)
CC	Contrasting Color
ch(s)	chain(s)
cm	centimeters
FPsc	Front Post single crochet(s)
FPhdc	Front Post half double crochet(s)
hdc	half double crochet(s)
hdc2tog	half double crochet 2 together
MC	Main Color
mm	millimeters
Rnd(s)	Round(s)
sc	single crochet(s)
sc2tog	single crochet 2 together
slip st2tog	slip stitch 2 together
sp(s)	space(s)
st(s)	stitch(es)
tr	treble crochet(s)
YO	yarn over

SYMBOLS & TERMS

★ — work instructions following ★ as any **more** times as indicated in addition to the first time.

( ) or [ ] — work enclosed instructions **as many** times as specified by the number immediately following **or** work all enclosed instructions in the stitch or space indicated **or** contains explanatory remarks.

colon (:) — the number(s) given after a colon at the end of a row or round denote(s) the number of stitches and spaces you should have on that row or round.

work even — work without increasing or decreasing in the established pattern.

GAUGE

Exact gauge is **essential** for proper fit. Before beginning your project, make the sample swatch given on page 6 in the yarn and hook specified. After completing the swatch, measure it, counting your stitches and rounds carefully. If your swatch is larger or smaller than specified, **make another, changing hook size to get the correct gauge**. Keep trying until you find the size hook that will give you the specified gauge.

CROCHET TERMINOLOGY

UNITED STATES		INTERNATIONAL
slip stitch (slip st)	=	single crochet (sc)
single crochet (sc)	=	double crochet (dc)
half double crochet (hdc)	=	half treble crochet (htr)
double crochet (dc)	=	treble crochet (tr)
treble crochet (tr)	=	double treble crochet (dtr)
double treble crochet (dtr)	=	triple treble crochet (ttr)
triple treble crochet (tr tr)	=	quadruple treble crochet (qtr)
skip	=	miss

Yarn Weight Symbol & Names	LACE 0	SUPER FINE 1	FINE 2	LIGHT 3	MEDIUM 4	BULKY 5	SUPER BULKY 6	JUMBO 7
Type of Yarns in Category	Fingering, size 10 crochet thread	Sock, Fingering, Baby	Sport, Baby	DK, Light Worsted	Worsted, Afghan, Aran	Chunky, Craft, Rug	Super Bulky, Roving	Jumbo, Roving
Crochet Gauge* Ranges in Single Crochet to 4" (10 cm)	32-42 sts**	21-32 sts	16-20 sts	12-17 sts	11-14 sts	8-11 sts	6-9 sts	5 sts and fewer
Advised Hook Size Range	Steel*** 6 to 8, Regular hook B-1	B-1 to E-4	E-4 to 7	7 to I-9	I-9 to K-10½	K-10½ to M/N-13	M/N-13 to Q	Q and larger

*GUIDELINES ONLY: The chart above reflects the most commonly used gauges and hook sizes for specific yarn categories.

** Lace weight yarns are usually crocheted with larger hooks to create lacy openwork patterns. Accordingly, a gauge range is difficult to determine. Always follow the gauge stated in your pattern.

*** Steel crochet hooks are sized differently from regular hooks–the higher the number, the smaller the hook, which is the reverse of regular hook sizing.

FOLLOWING A CHART

Designs for Fair Isle crochet are worked from a chart. It is easier to follow a chart than written instructions and you can also see what the pattern looks like. The chart shows each stitch as a square indicating what color each stitch should be. Visualize the chart as your fabric, beginning at the bottom edge of the chart.

If you crochet right-handed, follow the chart from **right** to **left**; if you crochet left-handed, follow the chart from **left** to **right**.

For ease in following the chart, place a ruler on the chart above the round being worked to help keep your place.

BLOCKING

Getting the yarn wet will make it softer and allow you to adjust the shape of the mittens. Try them on for size and fit, then take them off and rinse thoroughly with warm water, squeeze the excess water out (do **not** wring them out), roll them in a towel and squeeze again. Now you can lay them out flat on a drying rack to shape them by gently stretching and pulling them into the shape that you want and eliminate any twisting that may have occurred. Let dry completely before wearing.

MARKERS

Markers are used to help distinguish the beginning of each round being worked. When working split sc, place a split-ring marker **between** the vertical legs of the first stitch of each round *(Fig. 12)*, moving marker after each round is complete.

Fig. 12

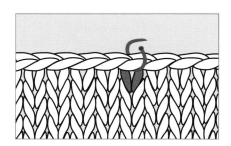

◖■□□□ BASIC		Projects using basic stitches. May include basic increases and decreases.
◖■■□□ EASY		Projects may include simple stitch patterns, color work, and/or shaping.
◖■■■□ INTERMEDIATE		Projects may include involved stitch patterns, color work, and/or shaping.
◖■■■■ COMPLEX		Projects may include complex stitch patterns, color work, and/or shaping using a variety of techniques and stitches simultaneously.

CROCHET HOOKS																
U.S.	B-1	C-2	D-3	E-4	F-5	G-6	7	H-8	I-9	J-10	K-10½	L-11	M/N-13	N/P-15	P/Q	Q	S
Metric - mm	2.25	2.75	3.25	3.5	3.75	4	4.5	5	5.5	6	6.5	8	9	10	15	16	19

BACK RIDGE

Work only in loops indicated by arrows *(Fig. 13)*.

Fig. 13

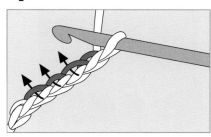

BACK OR FRONT LOOP ONLY

Work only in loop(s) indicated by arrow *(Fig. 14)*.

Fig. 14

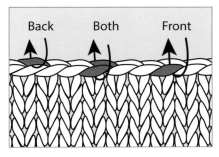

FREE LOOPS

After working in Back or Front Loops Only on a round, there will be a ridge of unused loops. These are called the free loops. Later, when instructed to work in the free loops of the same round, work in these loops *(Fig. 15a)*.

When instructed to work in free loops of a chain, work in loop indicated by arrow *(Fig. 15b)*.

Fig. 15a

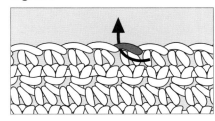

Fig. 15b

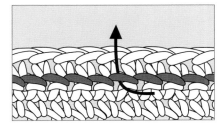

CHANGING COLORS

Insert hook in stitch indicated, YO and pull up a loop, place old yarn on top of previous round *(Fig. 16a)*, with new yarn, YO and draw through both loops on hook *(Fig. 16b)*.

Fig. 16a

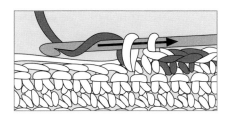

Fig. 16b

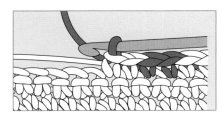

POST STITCH

Work around post of stitch indicated, inserting hook in direction of arrow *(Fig. 17)*.

Fig. 17

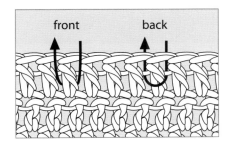

We have made every effort to ensure that these instructions are accurate and complete. We cannot, however, be responsible for human error, typographical mistakes, or variations in individual work.

Production Team: Instructional/ Technical Editor - Sarah J. Green; Senior Graphic Designer - Lora Puls; Graphic Designer - Janie Marie Wright; Photo Stylist - Lori Wenger; and Photographer - Jason Masters.

Library of Congress Control Number: 2018965107

Made in U.S.A.